Table (

MW01173837

Introduction

Wayne Rowland's life took a dramatic turn following an industrial accident, leading to a lifelong battle with lead poisoning and the development of stomach and esophagus cancer. Faced with a dire prognosis and the realization of his mortality, Rowland embarked on a quest for alternative treatments, ultimately uncovering innovative approaches to healing that have left an indelible mark on the field of holistic health.

Rowland's journey began with a pivotal encounter with Ray Schmidt, a Catholic priest, who introduced him to a unique remedy for lead poisoning. Dissatisfied with conventional treatments like surgeries and chemotherapy, Rowland sought unconventional paths to healing. His pursuit led him to explore suppressed cures for cancer, culminating in a $10,000 reward offered for information on alternative therapies.

The response was overwhelming, highlighting a widespread interest in unconventional healing methods. Through meticulous research and collaboration, Rowland discovered the work of Royal Rife and his groundbreaking frequency-based approach to treating cancer. Using Rife's technology, Rowland successfully eradicated his cancer and resolved other health issues, sparking a newfound passion for advancing alternative healing modalities.

Driven by his transformative experience, Rowland delved deeper into Rife's theories and the role of frequencies in health. He refined his understanding of frequency-based therapies and discovered the intricate but disturbing connection between parasites and disease. This revelation prompted a shift in focus from building Rife machines to addressing the root cause of illness: parasitic infestation.

Inspired by the explorative work of Nikola Tesla, Rowland embarked on a quest to harness the power of Tesla technology in holistic healing. His extensive collection of Tesla equipment became the cornerstone of his endeavors, leading to groundbreaking solutions such as a Tesla-lightning-induced colloidal silver.

Rejecting conventional colloidal silver formulations, Rowland sought to create a more potent and stable alternative using Tesla-inspired methods. By leveraging controlled lightning bolts and precise frequency modulation, he produced a revolutionary "Wain Water" product, later branded as "Silver Water." This innovative formulation represented a paradigm shift in holistic health, offering a reliable and effective solution for many ailments.

Despite his groundbreaking contributions, Rowland chose not to patent his creations, opting to share his knowledge and empower others to continue his legacy. His commitment to holistic healing and unwavering faith in the potential of innovative solutions continue to inspire generations of health enthusiasts and practitioners alike.

Wayne Rowland's journey exemplifies the power of resilience, ingenuity, and a relentless pursuit of truth in the face of adversity. His uniquely counter-intuitive contributions to holistic health represent the transformative potential of alternative therapies in promoting wellness and vitality.

This publication is intended for individuals who possess the capacity to manage their own well-being, approximately 10% of the population. It caters to those inclined to seek professional medical diagnosis when necessary but prefers to implement self-care strategies based on natural alternatives, contemporary scientific advancements, and minimally invasive procedures. Notably, these approaches entail abstaining from pharmaceutical interventions whenever possible.

This resource is not suitable for individuals grappling with dependencies on medical drugs, street drugs, tobacco, or alcohol. Until these addictions are overcome, self-help efforts may prove ineffective. In such cases, continued reliance on medical professionals is advised.

"A drug is a drug, no matter where you get it, and the human body is not suffering from a drug shortage."
~ Herb Roi Richards

Silver for Humans' Health, Wellness, and Healing

Chapter 1:

A Matter of Life and Death

Synopsis

In his own words, Wayne Rowland recounts his journey into the realm of alternative health innovations. He traces it back to a life-altering industrial accident that left him grappling with the enduring effects of lead poisoning and the scourge of cancer.

Confronted with a grim prognosis from conventional medical avenues, Rowland found himself at a crossroads, compelled to seek alternative paths to survival. As he embarked on his quest for answers, he discovered natural alternatives and the importance of frequency and developed Tesla lightning water.

A Matter of Life and Death

As a result of an industrial accident I was involved in, I suffer from lifelong lead poisoning and developed stomach and esophagus cancer, and I was dying. When my liver started to fail, I was told by the folks at the hospital that I was not going to survive this. I was put into a club called To Die with Dignity. I am a lifetime member and the only Survivor of our group. That was the first time I learned that love and forgiveness were essential in life if you want to survive.

Ray Schmidt, who was a Catholic priest, provided me with his horrible-tasting remedy and was able to help me get a grip on the lead poisoning. All my doctor had to offer were surgeries, chemotherapy, and radiation to buy me some time for my cancer. After conducting my research, I discovered that chemotherapy was mustard gas, and I thought to myself, there must be a better way.

$10,000 REWARD
for Suppressed Cancer Cure

I placed an ad in the newspaper in San Diego, and it read, my name is Wayne Roland. I am just like you. I have heard that there's a cure for the disease that has been suppressed. I have cancer. I'm not going to accept the modality of the day. I need to know if there's a suppressed cure, and I offer a ten-thousand-dollar reward.

Now, I'm in California. What do you suppose happened? I had to hire eight people to handle the phones in two shifts. I had to get eight phones installed. But one man called me. One man who impressed me and he said,

"There's not one cure for cancer that has been suppressed; there's been five. Which one do you want to know about?"

I said, "Whatever one works." He sent me to somebody who had an original Rife unit. I used it, and three months later, the cancer was gone. So was my arthritis.

I did it with frequency. This man, Royal Rife, had a microscope and invented this particular device in

1934. I bought one, used it, and got rid of my cancer, and I haven't had it since.

I was so gung-ho about it that I decided I had to get involved in building Rife machines and get it out there for people and help them.

So, I started researching the Rife technologies, and I found another man who knew quite a bit about Rife and had all the frequencies and everything. I went to see him and paid him a little bit of money, and he became a friend of mine.

I WASN'T EVEN USING THE RIGHT FREQUENCIES TO NEUTRALIZE CANCER

His name is John Sujaka; he showed me that I wasn't even using the correct hertz rate frequencies to get rid of cancer, not even close. That upset me because I paid good money for this! But why did the cancer leave?

I looked at the hertz rates that I was using, and lo and behold, the hertz rates I was using were to get rid of worms and parasites. It turned out that the lead poisoning was making a perfect bed for parasites to breed in furiously, and it was their waste that had given me cancer. I was absolutely in shock.

DISEASE IS CAUSED BY PARASITES

The more research I did, and the further I got into this, the more I discovered and concluded that worms and parasites cause all diseases.

So, I stopped building Rife equipment and selling it, and I wanted to find out what we could do about the worm and parasite issue.

I turned my attention to Nikola Tesla, and I searched for original pieces of his equipment.

I have probably the largest collection of Tesla equipment in the United States. I even bought some original Tesla equipment. I found original Tesla equipment in New York City in a basement that had been there for 48 years.

That's how I got into all the stuff I'm into with hertz rates and manufacturing lightning. Is there a method of finding a way to put these hertz rates into water? I needed it.

In a medical library in Seattle, I found a reference to a machine that produced lightning to create colloidal silver with lightning patented in the 1850s. This machine failed for its intended application, making colloidal silver for photographic processing, because they couldn't make it powerful enough.

But it looked like it would be powerful enough to do the job I wanted, especially if I could create a hybrid Tesla device. Since then, we've found a way not to make "colloidal silver" for your health because I disagree with putting ten parts per million of colloidal silver into a body. Too many long-term adverse effects have been discussed, and the discussions include a 40 percent failure rate in colloidal silver. The doctors who used it back in the day claimed that at one time, it would work, and at other times, it wouldn't.

So, I set out to make a Tesla lighting type of colloidal silver that was completely different and stable, with results that could be consistently depended on to work the same every time it was used. But wait, there's more.

While conducting my research, I became aware that the Earth is shifting off its axis. It's no longer vibrating at its extraordinary frequencies that play the music that keeps your body's vibration in a healthy state. And those frequencies are the musical notes that make up the major chord of B flat.

We created an electrical storm inside a giant Pyrex ball using Tesla technology. There are clouds in there with barometric readings that we monitor. We fire hertz rate-controlled bolts of lightning, one million two hundred thousand volts of kinetic energy, down a tube onto a pure piece of silver that is 99.99999 parts pure. That silver plate is as expensive as platinum.

These attenuated lightning bolts boil the molecules on the surface, and we spray clean distilled drinking water, like rain, onto the surface. The molecules explode into solution in angstrom sizes.

We control the field of flux around the tiny molecules of silver, so the silver starts to broadcast that into the solution, and voila, we have a Rife machine in water.

We learned how to control the hertz rate of a bolt of lightning, and we created three bolts with three different notes, the exact three notes that make up the B Flat chord, in the key of Earth vibrating at its most harmonious rate, B-flat, D, and F.

This Tesla lightning and B Flat major chord music-infused water was the birth of what I called Wain Water, which was commonly referred to as Music Water or Magic Water. I set up a manufacturing facility using my Tesla equipment and configuration to make the water using this process I developed in the 1980s.

I never patented it, but I set up a factory and empowered those I entrusted to make Silver Water using my trade secrets. At the same time, I continued to create and manifest by going to God's banquet table regularly.

Today, Wayne's "Wain Water" is simply branded, "Silver Water," and is shipped all over the country.

Chapter 2:

Silver Water

Synopsis

In this chapter, you will learn more about Silver Water, which, although a colloidal silver, is unlike any other commercially available or homemade colloidal silver on the market today.

Silver's broad-spectrum antimicrobial properties make it a potent alternative to synthetic antibiotics, capable of combating over 650 known diseases within minutes. Despite skepticism from the medical community, silver's unique mechanism of action and historical effectiveness fully support its therapeutic potential.

No other colloidal silver is made with Tesla lightning and is especially imbued with the B-flat major chord musical note frequencies, making this Silver Water unique.

Silver Water

While necessity is the mother of invention, a life-threatening circumstance can inspire one to take a new, proactive approach, especially if one's life depends on it, like Wayne's did.

Wayne's Silver Water is unlike any other known colloidal silver available on planet Earth. However, it has been likened to natural colloidal silver, the type that is made by none other than Mother Nature.

The only full-spectrum antibiotic, silver water, was discovered thousands of years before Greece and Rome during a previous high-tech civilization. Silver water was made using natural lightning during the Dark Ages, which always seems to occur between civilizations. When a storm approached, the village healer would set a silver container full of water on a local hill where lightning usually strikes. From a safe distance, she would watch to see if lightning struck it. If it did, she would bottle it up and use it as necessary to help heal her clients.

To make that same level of healing silver water today, Wayne Rowland made a high-tech lightning chamber using Tesla technology to duplicate that full-spectrum universal antibiotic used for thousands of years to kill all bacteria, viruses, yeast, and molds that cause disease in today's world.

The discharge of lightning is simply the only known way to get the tiniest flakes of electrically charged pure silver suspended in water to get maximum antibiotic action.

There are many standard methods of creating colloidal silver in the present day. Many products are marketed as "colloidal silver" and are available for purchase, often produced inexpensively by unqualified individuals operating from kitchen tables.

However, many of these purported colloidal silvers are essentially silver salts rather than actual colloidal silver solutions. Actual colloidal silver consists of minute silver particles suspended in pure distilled water through a process involving a strong electrical charge.

Consumers should be cautious of the imitations, as they lack the genuine properties of colloidal silver and may pose health risks. Silver salts, which comprise the majority of these products, have the potential to react unfavorably with chemicals in the body, leading to adverse effects. For instance, the accumulation of silver salts could result in the formation of silver platelets, posing a risk of severe conditions such as heart attacks. The FDA classifies silver salts as pesticides, while actual colloidal silver is recognized as a therapeutic aid.

Furthermore, the equipment utilized by some unregulated vendors resembles makeshift setups akin to homemade liquor distillation, lacking proper hygiene controls and the pure distilled water crucial for producing authentic colloidal silver.

Consuming such products not only risks wasting money but also jeopardizes one's health, potentially leading to long-term medical complications.

Consumers need to exercise discernment and prioritize their well-being when considering colloidal silver products, ensuring they seek out reputable sources with proven quality and safety standards.

Notably, as a common middle-school science project, a basic colloidal silver solution can even be made with as little as two silver electrodes hooked to three 9-volt batteries, but the silver flakes are much larger and less numerous, so they give off fewer of the silver ions that actually kill pathogens.

Making colloidal silver using batteries for your power source makes large chunks of silver too big to circulate through capillaries and get stuck, which can cause the silver to show through the skin, making the skin appear gray. If you attempt to create your own colloidal silver, use a higher current source to make your colloidal silver.

Colloidal Silver Quality Experiment

A straightforward experiment exists for assessing the quality of colloidal silver at home:

Pour a small quantity of the test liquid into a standard drinking glass, filling it up to approximately 2 inches or 5 centimeters.

Add one teaspoon of ordinary household salt to the liquid.

If the liquid remains clear after adding salt, it indicates that it is a proper colloidal silver solution. This clarity is attributed to the fact that the tiny silver particles do not react with salt. However, if the liquid becomes cloudy or milky, it suggests the presence of silver salts or additives such as stabilizers, possibly proteins.

While laboratories can perform more sophisticated tests like conductivity assessments and particle size analysis using electron microscopes, such resources may be limited to the average individual. Thus, the simple salt test serves as a practical and accessible means for determining whether a substance is indeed a colloidal solution or a potentially harmful silver salt.

Silver offers a powerful alternative, unlike most synthetic antibiotics, which typically target only around six types of germs and may become ineffective against resistant strains. Silver demonstrates broad-spectrum antimicrobial properties, capable of combating over 650 known diseases within a mere six minutes and without inducing any adverse side effects. Unlike artificial antibiotics, silver functions solely as a catalyst, refraining from engaging in chemical reactions with bodily tissues.

In Alfred B Searle's book "Use of Colloids in Health and Disease," the author asserts that colloidal silver possesses outstanding antimicrobial properties, capable of eradicating any known microbe within six minutes or less, even at concentrations as low as five parts per million.

Silver is characterized by its neutral taste, nearly odorless nature, and non-toxic properties. It has a long-standing reputation for compatibility with medical drugs and, in regular doses, poses minimal risk of stomach upset. Not only that, but silver also aids in digestion.

Silver's most notable attribute is its broad-spectrum effectiveness against various pathogens, including viruses, bacteria, yeast, mold, and fungus species. Remarkably, it is one of the few substances capable of reliably killing viruses, an accomplishment that has eluded conventional medical science with its artificial antibiotics.

Despite its demonstrated efficacy against pathogens, silver has not gained widespread acceptance or endorsement within the medical community for treating infectious diseases. This reluctance stems from several factors.

Firstly, many physicians are skeptical due to the need for robust scientific evidence, such as double-blind studies, supporting silver's efficacy.

Additionally, the absence of financial incentives, as silver is a natural substance without patent protection, further deters widespread adoption in favor of more lucrative patented antibiotics.

The unique mechanism of silver's action involves its catalytic effect on pathogens' oxygen-metabolizing enzymes. The presence of even a single silver particle in proximity to viruses, fungi, or bacteria swiftly eliminates their ability to utilize oxygen for metabolism. Consequently, these single-celled disease-causing agents suffocate and perish within minutes. This volatility substantiates silver's effectiveness in targeting a fundamental vulnerability shared by bacteria and viruses: their reliance on oxygen metabolism for survival and replication. By exploiting this vulnerability, silver interventions offer a potent means of combatting microbial threats with precision and efficacy.

Is it possible for fungi, bacteria, or viruses to develop resistance to colloidal silver?

According to extensive research over a century, the answer is a resounding no. Despite the prolonged presence of colloidal silver in various applications, there has never been a documented case of any organism developing resistance to it.

Resurrect Dying Flowers Home Experiment

To illustrate the life-giving/saving nature of Silver Water, consider this simple experiment:

Take two flowers from the same plant. Place one in a vase filled with water and leave the other on a bench for approximately eight hours. By the end of this period, the flower left on the bench will likely appear wilted and limp.

Now, fill another vase with colloidal silver and submerge the stem of the wilted flower, trimming the stem slightly since trimming the stem is necessary for absorbing the Silver Water.

The following day, you will observe the previously wilted flower standing upright again. Despite enduring significant stress and exhibiting signs of decline, the flower not only recovers but surpasses the longevity of the flower placed in regular water immediately.

This experiment accentuates the exceptional revitalizing properties of colloidal silver, suggesting a life-giving quality inherent to the silver colloid. Such observations further bolster the notion of Silver Waters' effectiveness as a potent antimicrobial agent without the risk of inducing resistance in pathogens.

Silver possesses potent antimicrobial properties, making it an effective agent for preventing infection when applied topically to cuts, scrapes, and open sores. Silver Water can be most effectively administered topically through the skin when combined with DMSO (dimethyl sulfoxide), which aids in its penetration for addressing internal issues.

As a result of his discoveries, Wayne Rowland observed miraculous outcomes in patients with severe burns. He recounts, "We've taken third-degree burn patients who've lost a third of an ear, had all the skin melted off their noses with only the cartilage sticking through, and third-degree burns all over at .047 parts per million, they just spray it on, and in six weeks the ear grows back without a scar to the total size that it is. So does the nose. So does all the flesh."

Expanding his efforts, Rowland extends his treatments to include children and a broader group of individuals. He shares, "One man lost all the flesh on his wrist and his hand and has lost the use of his hand completely. He sprayed the solution I built for him on that hand and regrew back the muscle tissue, nerves, and flesh without scarring."

Additionally, Rowland developed Silver Water Gel specifically formulated for individuals with scarring from old burns, yielding promising results. He explained, "And for those who have scarring from old burns, I built a Silver Water Gel so they could put it on, and we're having fantastic news about that, too."

Reflecting on the broader applications of his discoveries, Rowland suggested using his solution as a preventive measure for common ailments, "You'll find out you know if you feel a cold coming on grab a bottle of water and drink some. Knock it out." What quantity might be necessary? "If you got a cold coming on, a third of a bottle."

Wayne adds, "If you've got latent herpes in your body, take this Silver Water because the Silver Water will prevent the herpes from breaking out."

Another anecdote Rowland shares illustrates the effectiveness of Silver Water in treating severe conditions, "A lady in Chicago had this man-eating flesh disease that devours you in three days. I sent her overnight a case she just sprayed it on and drank the whole case, and then the next morning, she said she had never urinated so much in her life, but it was gone. It's single-celled, and they can't handle the music."

Regarding age suitability, Silver Water can be safely used by individuals of all ages, ranging from newly conceived embryos to pregnant mothers, newborns, children, and elderly individuals facing severe conditions such as cancer.

Silver's versatility extends to its application across various parts of the body. It can be taken orally, applied to the ears or eyes using a sprayer or dropper, sprayed or applied on soaked pads externally, utilized as a gel, administered via nebulizer for lung conditions, introduced into the bowel through an enema, or delivered intravaginally using a syringe. In emergencies, silver can even be injected directly into the bloodstream.

Due to its colloidal state or ionization, colloidal silver is readily absorbed in the mouth, throat, and stomach without causing harm to beneficial bacteria or enzymes in the intestines. This unique property ensures its antimicrobial effects are targeted while preserving the body's natural microbiome and digestive processes.

Wayne's Silver Water has been employed to tackle various health issues, from pneumonia and ear infections in children to colds, sore throats, allergies, and flu. Additionally, it is highly effective when applied to conditions like diabetes, hepatitis, chronic fatigue syndrome, arthritis, Lyme disease, hemorrhoids, prostate problems, yeast infections, herpes, syphilis, gonorrhea, canker sores, bad breath, and a range of skin ailments.

Remember cat scratches and animal bites. I mix up some DMSO and Silver Water and spray it on, which is the end of the problem. I've never had an infection if I spray it on soon after it happens. I usually use 1/3 Silver Water & 2/3 DMSO, so it will penetrate deep into the wound and eradicate any of the nasty bugs present.

For those who don't know, DMSO (dimethyl sulfoxide) is a natural herbal extract from trees. Trees use it to soak nutrients through rigid cellular walls, and humans use it to treat internal organs, muscles, and ligaments through the skin. When applied to the skin, most anything mixed with DMSO will be carried clear to the center of the bones.

The reason it soaks in like that is that it is starving for water, and it is constantly hunting for more water.

Chapter 3:
Silver Water and Disease

Synopsis

This chapter reviews the connection between silver water and disease elimination. Parasites and pathogens thrive in acidic, toxic environments, conceal themselves within biofilm, or change locations to evade detection. Chronic ailments and infectious diseases capitalize on such environments to manifest and increase.

Traditional medical approaches overlook the pervasive impact of parasites and bacteria on health, necessitating proactive intervention. Wayne Rowland's insights emphasize parasitic pathogens' prevalence and detrimental effects, advocating for customized treatment regimens to address their presence effectively.

Silver Water and Disease

Disease is an opportunistic aggressor, seeking openings to infiltrate, propagate, and flourish within unsuspecting hosts. By adopting a diet heavy in cooked and processed foods, characterized by acidity, oxidation, full of parasite eggs, and lacking genuine nutrients, we inadvertently cultivate an internal environment conducive to various forms of illness, both chronic and infectious. When sickness strikes, it is a clear indicator of our acidic and toxic state, as parasites and diseases flourish in acidic surroundings and feed on toxins. Therefore, these substances serve no functional purpose within the body and do not naturally belong.

When we foster an internal environment hostile to parasites and disease, they recoil and retreat, making you think that you've done your job defeating them, though this is merely an illusion of strength. Highly sophisticated parasites will hide in biofilm, change their address by moving to a new location in the body, and even hibernate to avoid detection. Chronic ailments manifest as internal assaults precipitated by the creation of a hospitable environment for disease within the body. Meanwhile, parasitic, bacterial, and viral infections represent external threats that capitalize on an internal ecosystem promoting their multiplication and expansion.

These parasitic pathogens find survival difficult in a body, maintaining proper hydration, alkalinity, and detoxification. By cultivating an environment characterized by these favorable conditions, we effectively dismantle the foundation upon which parasites, bacteria, and viruses thrive, threatening their continued existence.

A robust immune system promptly generates the necessary antibodies to combat invading pathogens. Alternatively, an immune system compromised by prolonged dehydration and inadequate nutrition cannot mount a defense against such assaults, as its ability to identify antigens is severely impaired. Without the ability to recognize pathogens, the body's immune system cannot produce the antibodies required to combat the encroaching disease and proliferation of parasites.

Like Wayne Rowland's own story about his reaching out for effective alternatives to a morbid health crisis for which there was no cure, anyone facing such a diagnosis might be well advised to seek a harmless frequency intervention by applying a regimen soaked in Silver Water as a potential solution.

The fundamental cause of various diseases can be attributed to pathogenic spirochetes and other bacteria, such as those implicated in strep throat, urinary tract infections, and tuberculosis. However, additional sources of illness, including viruses responsible for ailments ranging from the common cold to AIDS and fungi-causing conditions like ringworm and athlete's foot, further contribute to the spectrum of diseases. Parasites transmitted through mosquito bites, as seen in malaria cases, and other forms of parasites, present additional health risks.

Pathogenic spirochetes, known for their rapid spread of infectious diseases, are highly contagious, and often transmitted through direct contact. Contagion may occur from one individual to another through various means, including physical touch, respiratory droplets, or sexual contact. Contact with infected animals or their waste can also lead to illness, highlighting the potential dangers posed by indirect exposure.

Wayne often says, "If you have a pet, you need to deworm yourself, just like you do your pet, and if you don't have a pet, don't get one." They are famously the most common carrier of parasites and worms for the spreading among families and others today.

Insects acting as vectors, such as mosquitoes, fleas, and ticks, can also carry bacteria and parasites responsible for diseases like malaria and Lyme, further amplifying the risk of infection. Contaminated food and water serve as additional avenues for parasitic transmission, with pathogens like Escherichia coli (E. coli) posing health threats when ingested.

Furthermore, environmental toxins and metals contribute significantly to prevalent health conditions, infiltrating the body through various routes such as ingestion, inhalation, and skin contact.

Heavy metals like mercury and lead, notorious for their toxic effects on cells, are linked to a range of ailments, diseases, and disorders, including coronary artery disease and autoimmune disorders. Wayne's Parasite Cleanse & Deworming Program offers a comprehensive approach to identifying and removing these harmful substances, prioritizing individual safety and well-being.

Parasites play a pivotal role in the onset of various diseases, including cancer, infiltrating our bodies through inadvertent ingestion of parasite eggs present in our food. Some foods, like salad dressings that pick up trace amounts of alcohol throughout manufacturing, can facilitate hatching these eggs within our bodies.

Parasites target specific organs such as the pancreas and thymus, leading to conditions like diabetes, chronic fatigue syndrome, and fungal infections. In response, only an effective parasite cleanse and deworming regimen can eradicate parasites from the body, A secret held among ex-diabetics who have wholly overcome diabetes by doing so.

Many improvements are attributed to combatting parasites, such as enhancing vision through eye drops, applying Silver Water to the scalp, killing parasites, and resolving issues with hair loss.

Parasites are the stealthy perpetrators of illness, and the Parasite Cleanse & Deworming Program is proven time and time again to be the heralded solution to restoring overall vibrant health and increased longevity.

Parasites don't just steal our nutritious food, but they also crap in our bodies causing all manner of disease symptoms.

When observing individuals exhibiting disease symptoms, Wayne Rowland notes, "What I find is far more cunning and deceptive going on inside the human body of people who are really sick."

Recognizing the limitations of conventional medical approaches, Wayne emphasizes, "Doctors are limited to what they know, just as anyone is." His unique perspective, informed by his distinct course of study, afforded him insights not commonly acknowledged within traditional medical frameworks.

Rowland challenged prevailing notions about their prevalence and impact by identifying parasites, particularly worms, as a pervasive impediment to optimal health. He contends, "Even though the general consensus is that most of us are perfectly fine with living with these worms in a synergistic relationship, the fact remains that as they live inside you, you get sick when they urinate." Dismissing conventional skepticism, he asserts, "Doctors don't like to hear it, and the Food and Drug Administration of the United States will do whatever they can to keep you from thinking that any of this is true, even for a moment, and I don't really care."

Drawing from his firsthand observations, Rowland emphasizes, "This one thing I know; if I see worms prevalent in someone who has disease symptoms, the symptoms disappear after following my instructions."

In some cases, persistent symptoms may indicate the presence of pathogenic spirochetes, insidious bacteria with formidable adaptive capabilities.

Describing pathogenic spirochetes as "conscious parasitic bacterium," Rowland highlights their elusive nature and nefarious intent. He warned, "These microscopic enemies of human biology are internal terrorists hellbent on making you sick and keeping you suffering over a long period of time." Despite their stealth and resilience, Rowland maintained that intervention was possible, albeit challenging, indicating the necessity of individualized treatment approaches.

Intricate dynamics exist between the human body and its microbial adversaries, requiring a comprehensive understanding and proactive response to mitigate the impact of these treacherous pathogens.

More Than One Disease?

It is simply not typical for anyone to have a laundry list of diseases diagnosed one after the other or even at the same time unless they are being attacked from within by pathogenic spirochetes or evolving worms.

They are so highly versatile that they can appear to be the source of irritable bowel syndrome until they tire of medical IBS management protocols; then, they might morph into congenital heart disease. Try to mess with them, and they might turn into Multiple Sclerosis (M.S.), Amyotrophic Lateral Sclerosis (ALS), or Lou Gehrig's disease.

Despite the efforts of medical professionals, the limitations of traditional approaches abound in combating sequential disease variance.

All the while, your doctor does the best they can with the tools they have: run another blood test, evaluate the symptoms, make another diagnosis, and follow another method of managing the disease based on calculations and recommendations by the pharmaceutical industry. That is all you can expect from your doctor.

A more proactive solution would be to utilize a Disease Symptom Elimination Kit, tailored to target surviving pathogenic spirochetes, setting sights profoundly on these sophisticated, resilient pathogens as if declaring war on them.

It is imperative to pursue the elimination of pathogenic spirochetes and worms with consistency and diligence, as taking a break or faltering only gives them ample time to recalibrate, repopulate, and evolve, making the next go round even more difficult.

Chapter 4:

Gut Rebuilder Program

Synopsis

One of the best ways to fight off disease or any disorder is to have a healthy gut, the undeniable basis of a healthy immune system.

A powerful gut microbiome is crucial to overall health and wellness, influencing digestion, nutrient absorption, metabolism, and immune function. Mainstream medicine neglects the gut's importance, favoring pharmaceutical drugs and surgeries over natural approaches.

The program benefits patients undergoing medical treatments that harm gut flora and those seeking natural solutions. It addresses a wide range of conditions, including acne, autoimmune diseases, mood disorders, diabetes, and more.

Gut Rebuilder Program

People approach Wayne Rowland with an extensive range of health concerns. He discerns two primary categories of individuals: (1) those heavily reliant on conventional medical practitioners who prescribe specific therapies, and (2) those more self-reliant, assuming full responsibility for their well-being and often open to alternative approaches.

1. **Patients Under Medical Care**
2. **Independent Health Seekers**

Both groups stand to benefit significantly from an effective Gut Rebuilder Program. Patients under medical care, guided by doctors, may require enhanced gut health due to treatments that detrimentally affect it. The medical establishment's inclination toward therapies that harm gut flora, essential for bodily protection and repair, is highly suspect. It creates an environment propagating continued health decline by producing a breeding bed for parasites and disease.

When gut health is compromised, it likely necessitates additional medical intervention. However, addressing gut health naturally yields surprising results, potentially eliminating various health issues.

In the intricate landscape of human health, one often-overlooked hero stands tall: the gut microbiome. Despite its profound influence on our well-being, for some time mainstream medical science has turned a blind eye to its significance. Instead, the spotlight has been cast on man-made pharmaceutical drugs and invasive surgeries, neglecting the body's natural ability to heal itself through God-given means. However, a paradigm shift is underway, urging individuals to explore the wonders of rebuilding their gut naturally.

Your body comes pre-equipped with everything it needs to heal, repair, and regenerate, as necessary, if only the holistic system is cleaned, empowered, and maintained appropriately to do the work.

The gut microbiome, comprising trillions of microorganisms residing in our gastrointestinal tract, it is not just a passive bystander in our bodily functions. Instead, it plays a pivotal role in digestion, nutrient absorption, metabolism, and modulating our immune system. When this delicate balance is thrown into confusion, it can pave the way for a vast array of health issues ranging from digestive disorders to autoimmune diseases.

In recent years, scientific research has unveiled the intricate connections between the gut microbiome and overall health. Studies have linked dysbiosis, an imbalance in gut flora composition, to conditions such as inflammatory bowel disease (IBD), irritable bowel syndrome (IBS), gastroenteritis, obesity, diabetes, coronary heart disease, stroke, and even mental health disorders like clinical depression and anxiety. These findings call attention to the importance of nurturing a thriving gut ecosystem for optimal well-being.

Yet, conventional medicine often falls short in the rush for quick fixes. Pharmaceutical drugs may offer temporary relief, but they usually come with a barrage of side effects and do not even consider the root cause of the problem. Similarly, surgeries targeting the gastrointestinal tract may provide symptomatic relief but do nothing to address the underlying imbalance in the gut microbiome and cut down our ability to absorb essential nutrients.

This is where the natural approach shines. Rather than relying on synthetic interventions, individuals are encouraged to harness the power of nature to support gut health, which involves embracing a holistic lifestyle that nurtures the microbiome through parasitic management, dietary changes, stress management, adequate sleep, and regular exercise.

Diet serves as a cornerstone in nurturing a healthy gut microbiome. Incorporating a diverse array of whole foods rich in fiber, prebiotics, and probiotics can fuel the growth of beneficial bacteria while overpowering harmful pathogens. Fermented foods like yogurt, kefir, sauerkraut, and kimchi are particularly potent allies in this regard, delivering a hefty dose of beneficial microbes to the gut.

Reducing or eliminating the eating of processed foods, refined sugars, and artificial additives can help restore balance to the microbiome. These FDA-approved dietary culprits fuel the growth of harmful bacteria and contribute to chronic inflammation, further disrupting gut health.

In addition to changes in food strategies, managing one's stress levels is crucial for maintaining a harmonious gut ecosystem. The gut-brain axis is the communication system between the gut and the brain working both ways highlighting the profound impact of psychological stress on gut health. Meditation, yoga, deep breathing exercises, and time in nature can help alleviate stress and promote gut resilience.

Prioritizing quality sleep is also paramount for gut health. Sleep deprivation impairs immune function and disrupts the delicate balance of gut microbiota. Establishing a sleep schedule routine, creating a relaxing bedtime, and optimizing the sleep environment can work wonders in supporting gut health.

Lastly, regular physical activity has been shown to benefit the gut microbiome. Exercise promotes gut motility, enhances circulation, and modulates immune function, all contributing to a healthier gut environment.

Independent health seekers are often more attuned to holistic approaches and stand to gain from bolstering gut health, especially when undergoing rigorous detox programs that might otherwise compromise it.

The benefits of the Gut Rebuilder Program are multifaceted. It aids in rebuilding and regenerating the body, enhances the immune system, improves digestion, reduces inflammation, and boosts metabolism. Notably, it can enhance the metabolism of prescription medications, reducing side effects.

A less recognized benefit is the profound impact of gut health on mental health. Many treatment regimens adversely affect mental health, but optimal gut health can mitigate these effects, fostering energy, confidence, and cognitive function like never before.

The Gut Rebuilder Program is particularly beneficial for addressing a broad spectrum of conditions, including acne, autoimmune diseases, mood disorders, neurological disorders, diabetes, and skin diseases, among others, such as:

Acne
Allergic Rhinitis (hay fever)
Alopecia
Alzheimer's Disease
Antibiotic Therapy
Anxiety
Autism Spectrum Disorder
Autoimmune Diseases and Treatment
Celiac Disease
Chemotherapy
Chronic Fatigue Syndrome (CFS)
Chronic Illness Management
Chronic Kidney Disease (CKD)
Chronic Pelvic Pain Syndrome
Depression
Diverticulitis
Eczema
Fibromyalgia
Food Allergies and Sensitivities
Functional Dyspepsia
Gastroparesis
Heavy Metal Detoxification
Inflammatory Bowel Disease (IBD)
Irritable Bowel Syndrome (IBS)
Lupus
Lyme Disease
Metabolic Syndrome
Mood Disorders
Multiple Sclerosis
Neurological Disorders
Obesity
Parkinson's Disease
Psoriasis
Radiation Therapy
Rheumatoid Arthritis
Skin Diseases
Type 2 Diabetes
Vitiligo

to name a few.

Gut Rebuilder Program Components:

- 2 quarts of Silver Water
- 1 bottle of Ultrazyme Plus
- 1 container of Silver Water Greens
- 1 pound WR Dulse Seaweed
- 1 bottle of Ultrabiotic Plus
- 1 bottle of Bio-DynaZyme

Add Lugol's Iodine to the monthly supply, with a dosage of three drops daily. Note that Lugol's will not be required to be repurchased every month due to the low dosage that is necessary.

Note you will see the Gut Rebuilder Program as the basis for all Wayne's programs, as gut health is the primary foundation from which healing is conducted.

How to Conduct the Gut Rebuilder Program

1) First thing in the morning: Take three drops of Lugol's Iodine in 3 oz. of water. Do not take iodine if you are allergic to seafood. Then,

2) Wait at least 20 minutes before taking,

- 1 ounce Silver Water
- ½ ounce Stabilized Greens
- 5 capsules of Ultrazyme Plus
- 1 capsule Ultrabiotic Plus
- 1 capsule Bio-Dyna-Zyme

3) Mid-day: take

    3A: 20 minutes before eating lunch:

- 1 capsule Ultrabiotic Plus
- 2 capsules Ultrazyme Plus, if eating a mid-day lunch meal (subtract two from the evening)

Use Dulse seaweed throughout the day as food seasoning or garnish instead of salt.

3B: If no mid-day meal:

- 1 capsule Ultrabiotic Plus

Reminder: Use ½ oz. Dulse seaweed throughout the day as food seasoning or garnish in place of salt.

4) Evening: take the following any time, from 20 minutes before mealtime to at least 20 minutes before bedtime

- 1 ounce Silver Water
- 5 capsules of Ultrazyme Plus (3, if 2 taken mid-day before eating lunch)
- 1 capsule Ultrabiotic Plus
- 1 capsule Bio-Dyna-Zyme

Hint: If you are smoothie savvy, you could easily add the ingredients to a healthy shake.

Wayne Rowland's Gut Rebuilder Kit supports overall health and well-being and can help individuals better tolerate and recover from the rigors of treatment. Besides rebuilding the gut, the Gut Rebuilder Kit also rebuilds and strengthens blood and tissue, helps balance mood, and sharpens thought processes.

Think about the journey to optimal health as beginning within the gut. Rather than relying on pharmaceutical drugs or invasive procedures, you can take charge of your health and well-being using this gut protocol.

By nurturing a diverse and resilient gut microbiome, you can unlock the key to enhanced immunity, improved digestion, and overall vitality and longevity.

So, let us embark on this transformative journey towards a healthier, happier gut – and a healthier, happier life.

Chapter 5:

Parasite Cleanse & Deworming Program

Synopsis

In this chapter, you will learn how to kill worms and other parasites that make you sick. Reflecting on personal experiences, Wayne Rowland emphasizes parasites' insidious nature, invading the mind and specific organs like the pancreas to ensure their survival and perpetuation.

Rowland's extensive experience treating various health conditions with deworming regimens and Silver Water demonstrates impressive efficacy in improving health outcomes, including cases of leukemia and lupus.

Parasite Cleanse & Deworming Program

Wayne Rowland embarked on a journey through medical literature dating back to the 1800s, unearthing a trove of deworming programs and detailed depictions of parasites prevalent in human tissues. Reflecting on this discovery, Rowland remarked, "Out of every single book were deworming programs, parasite programs all through the Americas and all through the world, parasite programs, and pictures of parasites that they had found in flesh."

Despite the historical prevalence of these programs, modern medical professionals are dismissive of parasite concerns, attributing them solely to regions deemed "third-world countries."

Wayne Rowland challenges the pompous American medical skepticism about parasites by seeking out individuals who rely on alternative methods like applied kinesiology, muscle testing, and pendulum work to assess parasite presence.

Dismissing their conclusions, Rowland noted, "I went to them, and I said, 'Do people have parasites?' They did pendulum work and came up with the answer, 'No.' I said Okay.

"Regardless of their results, I want to tell you, every single person that's used a pendulum on a person, concluded that he or she was parasite-free."

Applied kinesiology, muscle testing, and pendulum work produce errant results because these techniques rely on connecting to a higher energy source to answer your queries.

Unfortunately, parasites, particularly worms and pathogenic spirochetes, are highly intelligent survivalists and hackers of the human genome. They know how to access and manipulate human biology to survive.

These advanced, highly evolved parasites also invade the mind to protect themselves. They will block access to or alter the results of your energetic queries as a self-defense survival tactic.

Drawing from personal experience, Rowland recounts his own encounter with parasites, initially mistaking them for mucus until observing their activity in warm water. This revelation spurred him to develop a substance to facilitate the deworming process.

You Are a Parasite Farm

Rowland emphatically asserts about parasites' use of our bodies, "They're farming in you! Can you imagine?" He explains, "If that's a conscious state and a parasite finds out that a woman is now going to have a child, and the child's now getting all the special enzymes and all the special things through the mother-to-be, what does that parasite do? The parasites get on a pile of filth, travel up into the brain, and always know exactly where to lean against the wall, throwing her into cravings for food they want, rather than what's good for the developing child."

Complex interactions exist between parasites and the immune system, enabling parasites to evade and exploit the body's immune responses and cause harm.

Considering these insights, Rowland emphasizes the significance of addressing parasitic infestations, highlighting their potential impact on physiological processes and the health of the holistic individual.

Wayne Rowland has a wealth of insights into the intricacies of parasitic infections and their impact on human health, explaining the importance of prioritizing parasite elimination before embarking on any intestinal cleanse or dietary regimen, "Never do an intestinal cleanse or a diet before you kill parasites," he cautions, stressing the detrimental effects of parasites on gut health. Rowland points out the risk of developing leaky bowel syndrome if parasites are not addressed first.

Regarding maintenance after deworming, Rowland advocates for an annual deworming regimen as a preventive measure against reinfection. He emphasizes the perpetual presence of parasites in the environment and the need for consistent vigilance. "Once you've managed to put yourself under control and put a stop sign up for the parasites, they're always going to be around," he remarks, advocating for an annual deworming routine to maintain optimal health.

Rowland continually delves into the unsuspected sources of parasitic infection and highlights the prevalence of parasite eggs in soil and water.

You risk getting infected by consuming contaminated produce, particularly salad greens, and surprisingly, parasite eggs present in salad dressing could hatch in the human gut, leading to various health issues.

Your body, organs, and their functioning are at risk and constantly under attack by parasites, including worms, and other parasitic infections. Though some of them can be seen with the naked eye, most are microscopic, but the adverse effects they cause on the human body are immense as they grow in size and population. One of the organs primarily at risk is the pancreas.

Parasites disrupt normal physiological processes, leading to conditions like diabetes. "Your pancreas stores wood alcohol to save you from it," Wayne explains, linking parasitic presence to the development of diabetes and other health issues. Wood alcohol is often a poisonous additive that finds its way into processed food.

When at risk, parasites seek refuge in specific organs like the pancreas, especially if they sense an environment supporting their continued survivability. This leads to further potential consequences of parasitic infiltration into vital organs.

Due to our current understanding of parasitic dynamics, we've developed a comprehensive deworming program to address parasitic infections and their associated health complications.

Many success stories exist of individuals who have overcome diabetes through this program. "I've got thousands of diabetics that are no longer diabetics," Wayne proudly states, in support of the transformative effects of deworming on health outcomes.

Even though Wayne Rowland doesn't sell the products himself, he offered a full refund of every penny spent, out of his own pocket, to any diabetic who took his 10-case Silver Water challenge and did not overcome their diabetic condition. The challenge consisted of drinking 8 ounces or more of Silver

Water per day, conducting the Parasite Cleanse & Deworming Program for the first three months, and continuing to take whatever might be left until the 10 cases and any other products were gone, and so was their diabetes, "because no one ever claimed a refund. Not one."

Look at the connection between parasitic infestations and conditions like chronic fatigue syndrome and Candida overgrowth. Parasites disrupt thymus function, leading to systemic health issues. Wayne explains, "When they get into your thymus, your thymus starts to shut down," highlighting the far-reaching consequences of these oft-overlooked parasitic infections.

Wayne Rowland's wealth of experience treating various health conditions, including leukemia, lupus, and multiple sclerosis (M.S.), with deworming regimens and Silver Water is striking. "And then we get to leukemia, and we get to lupus," he recounts, emphasizing the transformative effects of his approach on terminal patients. The efficacy of deworming cannot be denied, especially in treating those with leukemia and lupus. Remarkably, eliminating parasitic infestations eliminated the disease, "Leukemia and lupus, it knocks 'em out. Just annihilates them once and for all," he affirms, emphasizing the profound impact of addressing underlying parasitic burdens.

When Rowland speaks, he will likely share anecdotes of individuals experiencing significant improvements after undergoing deworming treatments. He recounts the case of a woman who expelled astonishingly large parasites from her body, vividly describing them as "18-inch-long critters" of various shapes and sizes. Rowland's observations emphasize the diverse manifestations of parasitic infections and the need for comprehensive treatment strategies.

Reflecting on his extensive experience, Rowland positively affirms the universal benefits reported by individuals post-deworming. "And every single person I have dewormed, I have never yet dewormed anyone where they didn't tell me 'Hey, I feel 25 percent better'," as an example of the consistent, inspiring outcomes observed in his practice.

There are lesser-known indicators of parasitic infections, such as halitosis and ammonia levels in the blood. Bad breath is a telltale sign of heavy parasitic infestations attributed to "worm urine and droppings." Rowland's insights into the correlation between ammonia levels and parasitic activity provide valuable diagnostic clues for identifying parasitic burdens in individuals.

In Wayne Rowland's extensive experience, he drives home a fundamental truth: ***nobody is immune to the presence of worms and parasites.***

Reflecting on historical practices, Rowland draws attention to the approaches taken by doctors in the 1800s, particularly referencing the work of Dr. Chase from Chicago. "What did the doctors do when they dewormed you?" he ponders, highlighting the prevalence of primitive and unglamorous deworming remedies documented in Dr. Chase's books.

We all should be as impressed by Dr. Chase's remarkable findings as Wayne Rowland is. Chase notes that individuals who adhered to regular deworming schedules experienced better health outcomes than those who did not. "I have asked everybody how often they deworm, and the people that deworm every year never come in for anything," Rowland quotes from Dr. Chase's records. He further highlights Dr. Chase's success in treating cancer through deworming, citing an impressive 80% success rate in Chicago during the 1800s.

Continuing his narrative, Rowland addressed the challenges of diagnosing parasitic infestations, cautioning against reliance on methods like muscle testing. "A parasite program is a poison. Are you going to test good for a poison? No, never," he asserts, challenging the efficacy of applied kinesthetics and muscle testing in detecting parasitic infections and querying regarding what interventions might or might not be of value.

Driven by a desire to understand the phenomenon of parasitic infections more deeply, Rowland embarked on his deworming journey first, "So, I did myself first, and lo and behold," he recounts, describing his startling discovery of eight to ten-inch parasites expelled from his body. This personal experience prompted Rowland to extend his deworming efforts to a broader audience, ultimately treating a staggering several hundred thousand individuals since then.

There have been many stories and testimonials attesting to the profound impact of parasite elimination on individuals' health and well-being. Rowland's commitment to addressing parasitic infections demonstrates his dedication to improving the health of those he serves.

Rowland's expertise in deworming therapies and his profound understanding of parasitic dynamics offer hope and healing to countless individuals grappling with complex health conditions. His holistic approach and dedication to addressing underlying parasitic infections exemplify his commitment to improving the well-being of his patients.

The Parasite Deworming Program

The following is Wayne's Basic Parasite Deworming Kit, also known as the Clean Me Up Program.

Ingredients required for a one-month Basic Parasite Deworming Kit:
- 8 quarts of Silver Water
- Ultrazyme Plus
- WR Dulse Seaweed
- Silver Water Greens 15 ounces
- Lugol's Iodine

Add to the basic kit your choice of dewormer, available from veterinarians or farm stores. There are three primary varieties:

1. Benzimidazoles (brand names end in "ole" like mebendazole or fenbendazole).
2. Pyrimidines (brand names begin with "py" and in pyrantel).
3. Macrocyclic lactones (brand names end in "tin" such as ivermectin or moxidectin).

Caution: Dewormers are good for killing worms but also threaten the balance of an otherwise healthy gut.

Therefore, do not take any dewormer without supplementing to maintain a healthy, balanced microbiome (included in the basic parasite deworming kit). Note that the Gut Rebuilder Kit is essential to any other program, especially if it features an otherwise harmful ingredient, like a heavy-duty dewormer.

Dewormer Rotation: If you conduct the entire program over three months, David M Masters suggests rotating the type of dewormer (ole/py/tin) each month, as each one attacks the worms differently. Switching up the killing methods helps to change the frequency of the protocol and prevents the creation of dewormer-resistant strains of worms, which can happen if you administer only one type. You do not want to create further evolving super-worms.

What About Over-the-Counter Deworming?

Yes, there are herbal-based dewormers that can reduce worm populations somewhat. On their own, the effects are minimal in comparison to the heavy-duty commercial dewormers noted previously. According to Wayne Rowland, these health food store varieties of worm programs can increase the efficacy of the Parasite Deworming Program. How?

Wayne says that if, as Nikola Tesla said, everything is energy, frequency, and vibration (and it is), then these herbal worm concoctions help change the frequency of the parasite deworming program because every concoction has its own frequency. Therefore, regularly integrating one of them for the later 15 days of the month regularly will change the energy and vibration of the program, so it will make the parasites more vulnerable. The change in frequency throws them off-guard disrupting their evasion strategies. If you are doing this for three months, it would be good to change the herbal concoction each month as well, to keep the energy unfamiliar to the parasites being targeted, thereby increasing their death rate.

How Often Should I Deworm?

One will feel positive results after just one week of conducting the Parasite Deworming Program. Better results are experienced by diligently moving through the program every day for the full 30 days.

The best results are experienced by conducting the Parasite Deworming Program for three consecutive months, especially for those troubled by disease symptoms.

After that, a one-month Parasite Deworming Program may be conducted whenever necessary or suggested by your professional natural alternative specialist. Frequency varies from once a season to once a year, depending on individual circumstances. Wayne Rowland recommends a one-month program once a year unless you are addressing a more severe condition, in which case a more frequent program may be necessary.

Advanced Parasite Deworming Add-ons

Wayne Rowland and other natural alternative specialists may suggest an advanced approach to one's parasite cleanse and deworming depending on the needs of the individual.

Advanced additional products may include:

- Ultrabiotic Plus
- Bio-DynaZyme
- Serrapeptase

An advanced approach may be necessary if the individual does not have a robust microbiome or has considerable health challenges before beginning the program.

Chapter 6:

Disease Symptom Elimination

Synopsis

As evidenced by the works of Wayne Rowland and Herb Roi Richards, the path to disease symptom elimination is straightforward. It revolves around addressing pathogens, parasites, and worms, rebuilding the immune system, and adopting a healthier lifestyle. Individuals can take significant steps towards eliminating disease symptoms by avoiding pathogenic, poisonous, or processed foods and reducing exposure to toxins.

The Disease Symptom Elimination Kit outlined by Wayne Rowland offers a comprehensive approach to restoring health and well-being. With a combination of Silver Water colloidal, DMSO, chlorine dioxide, and other supplements, individuals can effectively support their body's natural healing processes and eliminate disease symptoms.

Disease Symptom Elimination

In today's world, the prevalence of diseases is ever-increasing. From chronic conditions to acute illnesses, the spectrum of ailments afflicting individuals is vast and seemingly endless. However, delving into history, we find a stark contrast: there was a time when diseases were not as rampant as today. Instead, people would present with specific symptoms, seeking remedies or natural health suggestions to alleviate their discomfort.

The evolution from symptom-focused healthcare to disease-centric medical practices is worth examining. In the past, individuals would seek treatment for a particular symptom, such as pain, inflammation, or digestive issues. Doctors would provide personalized remedies or lifestyle adjustments to address these symptoms effectively. However, in contemporary medicine, the landscape has shifted dramatically.

Today, the spread of diseases can be attributed to the influence of pharmaceutical companies. Rather than addressing individual symptoms, modern medicine tends to categorize symptoms into predetermined disease labels. This approach enables doctors to input a set of symptoms into a computer, generating a corresponding disease diagnosis along with recommended pharmaceutical interventions or surgical procedures. While this method may seem efficient, it raises pertinent questions about the integrity of healthcare and the role of medical professionals.

> *"I don't care what name you put on it, just get rid of the problem."*
> ~ *Herb Roi Richards*

One of the primary concerns with this disease-centric model is the emphasis on symptom management rather than holistic healing. Instead of focusing on treating the root cause of the symptoms, the medical system often prioritizes the suppression of manifestations through medication or surgery. This approach may provide temporary relief but does not address the underlying issues contributing to the symptoms.

If you have yet to notice, reliance on pharmaceutical

and surgical interventions comes at a significant cost. Patients are frequently subjected to financially extravagant treatments, medications, and procedures, leading to a cycle of dependency on the healthcare system. Thereby, The American medical industry profits from the perpetuation of diseases rather than the pursuit of genuine healing or cure.

So, what is the alternative?

Shifting the paradigm from disease management to actual symptom elimination is imperative for restoring the integrity of healthcare. Instead of merely masking symptoms with medication, the focus should be on identifying and addressing the underlying causes of the illness. This approach requires comprehension of the interconnectedness of physical, mental, and emotional health.

Holistic modalities, including parasite elimination and nutrition, lifestyle modifications, stress management, and alternative therapies, play a pivotal role in disease symptom elimination. That is what you really want to do; is it not? The mainstream on the other hand seems to want you to keep and control your disease rather than totally get rid of it.

By addressing factors such as exposure to pathogens, poor diet, sedentary lifestyle, environmental toxins, and emotional stressors, individuals can support their body's innate ability to heal and thrive.

According to Wayne Rowland and Herb Roi Richards, the path to disease symptom elimination is simple. The easy answer is, "It's all about the pathogens, parasites, and worms, rebuilding one's immune system by reestablishing a healthy microbiome, and living a healthier lifestyle, such as avoiding pathogenic, poisonous, or processed food and exposure to toxins."

As you may have noticed in this work, in most cases, if not all, a medical victim's complaints can be remedied by following any of Wayne Rowland's recommendations provided herein.

Disease Symptom Elimination Kit

The following is Wayne's Disease Symptom Elimination program.

Ingredients required for a one-month Disease Symptom Elimination Kit:

- 3 quarts of Silver Water
- Ultrazyme Plus
- WR Dulse Seaweed
- Silver Water Greens 15 ounces
- DMSO
- Chlorine Dioxide
- Lugol's Iodine

Add to the basic kit, your choice of dewormer, available from veterinarians or farm stores. There are three basic varieties:

1. Benzimidazoles (brand names end in "ole" like mebendazole or fenbendazole).
2. Pyrimidines (brand names begin with "py" as in pyrantel).
3. Macrocyclic lactones (brand names end in "tin" such as ivermectin or moxidectin).

How to Conduct Disease Symptom Elimination

1) First thing in the morning: take three drops of Lugol's Iodine in 3 oz. of water. Do not take iodine if you are allergic to seafood. Then,

2) Wait at least 20 minutes before taking,

- 1 ounce Silver Water
- 1 teaspoon DMSO
- ½ ounce Stabilized Greens
- 5 capsules of Ultrazyme Plus
- 1 capsule Ultrabiotic Plus
- 1 capsule Bio-Dyna-Zyme

3) Mid-day: take,

  3A: 20 minutes before eating lunch:

  - 1 ounce Silver Water
  - 1 teaspoon DMSO
  - 1 capsule Ultrabiotic Plus

- 2 capsules Ultrazyme Plus, If eating a mid-day lunch meal (subtract 2 from evening)

Use Dulse seaweed throughout the day as food seasoning or garnish instead of salt

3B: If no mid-day meal:

- 1 ounce Silver Water
- 1 teaspoon DMSO
- 1 capsule Ultrabiotic Plus

Reminder: Use ½ oz. Dulse seaweed throughout the day as food seasoning or garnish in place of salt.

4) Evening: take the following any time, from 20 minutes before mealtime to at least 20 minutes before bedtime

- 1 ounce Silver Water
- 1 teaspoon DMSO
- 5 capsules of Ultrazyme Plus (3, if 2 taken mid-day before eating lunch)
- 1 capsule Ultrabiotic Plus

- 1 capsule Bio-Dyna-Zyme

Hint: If you are smoothie savvy, you could easily add the ingredients to a healthy shake.

How to Make and Take Chlorine Dioxide

Use a simple two-part water purification drops kit that is readily available to make chlorine dioxide. These directions are for the two-part kit with the following specifications only: 1 bottle of Sodium Chlorite 28% four fl. oz. and 1 citric acid 50%/50% distilled water liquid four fl. oz.

Follow the directions that come with your chlorine dioxide water purification drops. In a clean, dry glass, three drops of Part 1 or Part A (sodium chlorite solution) are added to three drops of Part 2 or Part B (citric acid solution). Swirl drops together and allow activation for 30 to 40 seconds, then add 4 ounces of pure (distilled preferred) water. Swirl and drink quickly.

Do this once an hour every hour for 8 to 10 hours, except for not taking a chloride dioxide dose the hour of and the hour following the Silver Water dose.

Note Chlorine Dioxide Tolerance Test: It is suggested that individuals start with one drop each. If tolerated, take two drops the next hour, then three in the third hour. If a negative side effect is experienced, reduce the dose to 1/2 and 1/2 again (1/4 drop) if necessary, then work your way up incrementally as you can until you reach the three-drop dose. To make a half-drop, add 8 ounces of water and pour off 4 ounces to take and discard the rest. To make a 1/4 drop, add 16 ounces of water, pour off four ounces to take and discard the remainder.

How to Make Up 1 Quart per Day: Mix up to 24 drops Part 1 or A to up to 24 drops Part 2 or B in a clean, dry glass, swirl, and allow to activate for 30 to 40 seconds. Add to 32 ounces of distilled water. Make it in the morning and drink 4 ounces every hour throughout the day; store it in a high-quality (PET) plastic glass or glass container. Many sealable sports bottles are marked off in eight increments. Every hour just drink down to the next mark. Keep the solution in a cool, dry place away from direct sunlight; this batch will last 10 hours if kept sealed. Make a new batch on the next day. Throw out any left from the day before.

CDS 3000: Alternatively, you could use CDS 3000 (Chlorine Dioxide 3,000 PPM), which is already mixed and ready to use. Take 1/4 ounce added to 4 ounces of distilled water every hour. (DIY Tip: See the Internet for How to Make CDS 3000 if inclined.) Since CDS 3000 is so pure (manufactured via a distillation process), there is less likely to be a detox/herxheimer effect. If there is, just as in the 2-part kit, reduce the dose by half (double the water & take half, etc.).

TIPS: Disease Symptom Elimination

Dewormer:

Get 1 of the three dewormers (ole/py/tin). Take the first dewormer on the first of the month and the fifteenth. Rotate to the second brand of dewormer for the next month on the same days, the 1st and 15th. Switch to the third brand, take on the 1st and 15th of the third month. It doesn't matter in which order you rotate them. Only use dewormers for the first three months, then discontinue unless you are actively aware of your deworming process and are sure that you require additional deworming. Then, conduct a second round in months 4, 5, and 6. See more information about dewormers in Chapter 5's Parasite

Cleanse & Deworming Program.

Silver Water and DMSO:
Pour 1 ounce of Silver Water into a shot glass, add one teaspoon of DMSO to the shot glass, and take together in one shot. Allow to work for two hours before taking chlorine dioxide.

Use the Disease Symptom Elimination program to release yourself from any disease symptoms, no matter what diagnosis you may have been pharmaceutically-labeled with. Continue until you are entirely free of the symptoms, then continue for at least one additional week.

The Time Has Come

Empowering individuals to take the leading role in their healthcare is essential. Education, prevention, and self-care practices can significantly reduce the incidence of diseases and promote overall well-being. By contributing to the establishment of symbiotic collaboration between patients and their healthcare providers, the focus can shift from disease management to true healing and prevention.

The current disease-centric medical model perpetuates a cycle of symptom management and pharmaceutical dependency. To truly transform healthcare, we must prioritize symptom elimination through holistic approaches that address the root causes of illness. By shifting our focus from managing diseases to promoting healing and wellness, we can create a healthcare system that prioritizes the symbiotic well-being of individuals over the medical industries' parasitic profits.

Chapter 7:

Doctors and the FDA

Synopsis

In this chapter, you will find out about doctors, the case for silver, and how the FDA stands in the gap, preventing Americans from taking full advantage of and having access to Silver Water and other colloidal silvers.

Doctors, indoctrinated within medical schools, are trained to view parasitic infections as distant concerns, leading to skepticism and misdiagnoses when patients present symptoms of parasite infestation.

The FDA's cautionary stance on colloidal silver reflects pharmaceutical industry influence and regulatory hurdles despite centuries of historical efficacy and files full of anecdotal evidence supporting its benefits.

Doctors and the FDA

In modern American medicine, mentioning parasites and worms within the human body often triggers skepticism, if not outright dismissal. Across medical circles in the United States, there exists a prevailing notion that such issues belong solely to the domain of third-world countries, a relic of the past that has been eradicated in developed nations. Yet, this dismissal may come at a grave cost, as mounting evidence suggests that parasites such as worms could significantly contribute to various health ailments, challenging conventional medical wisdom.

Doctors, the supposed gatekeepers of healthcare, are not immune to this prevailing mindset. Medical professionals trained within the confines of drug company-controlled medical schools are conned into believing parasitic infections are a distant concern, scarcely relevant to their American patients. As a result, when individuals present symptoms indicative of parasitic infestations, they are often met with skepticism and disbelief. Such encounters can lead to misdiagnoses, with conditions like Morgellon's disease—a contentious diagnosis associated with delusional parasitosis—being assigned instead.

It's understandable why doctors might adopt such a stance. After all, the statistics provided to the medical community suggest that the prevalence of parasitic infections in the United States is minimal compared to regions with inadequate sanitation and healthcare infrastructure. Consider also that the symptoms of parasitic infections can often mimic those of other more common ailments, making diagnosis challenging without clear epidemiological indicators.

However, dismissing the possibility of parasitic involvement in disease processes is a grave oversight. Emerging research indicates that parasites including worms play a far more significant role in human health than previously acknowledged. Some experts even go as far as to suggest that all diseases can be traced back to pathogens or parasites, challenging the fundamental understanding of illness within contemporary medicine.

While the idea may seem old-fashioned, there is mounting evidence to support the role of parasites in chronic conditions such as autoimmune disorders, gastrointestinal ailments, and even mental health disorders. Parasites have evolved intricate mechanisms to evade detection by the immune system, often establishing long-term, synergistic relationships with their hosts. In doing so, they can manipulate immune responses and disrupt physiological processes, potentially leading to myriad health complications.

Herb Roi Richards' made the acquaintance of a former heart surgeon. Due to his youthful appearance, Herb thought he was too young to have retired, so he asked him why he was no longer actively a heart surgeon. And the man replied, "I just couldn't do it anymore." He explained, "I often would find patients' hearts full of worms, and when I asked my superiors what to do about it. I was instructed to pull the worms out." He was further ordered to sew them back up and never to mention the worms to anyone. This broke the young surgeon's heart, and he decided to leave the profession rather than live a lie. He was sure he would have to participate in other lies and deception if he stayed on. He thought himself better off by cutting his losses and quitting his job.

The reluctance of mainstream medicine to entertain the notion of parasitic involvement in disease processes exposes a broader issue within the healthcare system: the tendency to prioritize pharmaceutical interventions over holistic approaches. In an era dominated by the pharmaceutical industry, which thrives on treating symptoms rather than addressing root causes, the idea of parasites as a pervasive health threat may seem incongruent with the prevailing narrative.

However, as the field of microbiome research continues to evolve, our understanding of the intricate relationship between humans and their microbial inhabitants deepens. The human body is teeming with microorganisms, many of which play crucial roles in maintaining health. Yet, disruptions to this delicate balance, whether through antibiotic use, dietary choices, or environmental factors, can pave the way for opportunistic pathogens, including parasites, to thrive.

Addressing the issue of parasitic infections in America requires a paradigm shift within the medical community—one that embraces a more holistic approach to healthcare. Rather than patently dismissing patient concerns, doctors should adopt a more open-minded perspective, considering the possibility of parasitic involvement in disease processes. This may entail incorporating comprehensive diagnostic protocols, including stool analyses and serological testing, to detect parasitic infections accurately.

It is important to note that educating healthcare professionals and the general public about the prevalence and potential consequences of parasitic infections is paramount. By raising awareness and creating an environment aligned with personal holistic vigilance, we can empower individuals to take proactive measures to administer their own health and seek outside medical support only when necessary.

Wayne often cites the Veterinary Parasitology Reference Manual by William J. Foreyt regarding parasite life cycles which includes sections on laboratory animal parasites and human parasites.

The notion of parasites and worms as a health threat in America may seem inconceivable in modern medicine. Yet, dismissing their significance could be a grave oversight with far-reaching consequences. By challenging entrenched beliefs and adopting a more holistic approach to healthcare, we can better address the complex interplay between parasites and human health, paving the way for improved outcomes and a healthier future.

Wayne Rowland notes the prevailing attitude among doctors, "Doctors don't think that they have a problem. And that's why they die at what? 58? That's their lifespan?" He emphasizes the grim reality, stating, "While dead doctors don't lie, you know they're dead." Wayne referenced a notable book titled "Dead Doctors Don't Lie," by Dr. Joel D. Wallach, acknowledging its accuracy with the assertion, "They don't lie. They're dead."

Furthermore, Wayne highlights the detrimental consequences of neglecting proper nutrition: "They starve to death. They get old. They refuse to feed their bodies the nutrient values they need."

Dr. Joel D. Wallach, a renowned advocate for nutritional approaches to health, poses thought-provoking questions regarding modern medicine and its practitioners' health. "If medicines prevent death, and if doctors knew how to help you, then why are all the doctors dying from the same diseases they're treating you for?" Dr. Wallach queries, challenging the prevailing notions surrounding medical interventions and mortality rates among healthcare professionals.

A look at the mortality rate of medical practitioners causes one to ponder why doctors die at an age that precedes their patients. Especially since we are expected to believe they are responsible for being the guardians of the information and technology that is supposed to prolong a healthy life. It makes you wonder.

Drawing attention to the paradoxical nature of physician health, Dr. Wallach raises poignant examples: "Why do cardiologists drop dead from heart attacks? Why do psychiatrists kill themselves?" These questions accentuate a more profound concern regarding the efficacy of conventional medical practices in addressing chronic health conditions, even among those tasked with their management and treatment.

Throughout his career, Dr. Wallach has amassed a collection of obituaries detailing the untimely deaths of medical professionals. This somber archive is a testament to mainstream medicine's inadequacies in safeguarding its practitioners' well-being. However, Dr. Wallach juxtaposes this grim reality with a striking observation: "But veterinarians cure these same diseases in animals with nutrition and vitamins because animals don't have Blue Cross, Blue Shield, Medicare, and Medicaid, that's why."

Another point is that the farmer does not call that veterinarian again if the animals die. Human health care is just the opposite; It is to the doctor's benefit to keep you from getting over a long-term illness. Otherwise, he only sees you once. In other words, the doctor must be incentivized to help you overcome your problem. Now, he makes out better if you have a lifelong illness.

This comparison sheds light on the disparity between veterinary medicine, which often emphasizes nutritional interventions, and human healthcare, which predominantly relies on pharmaceutical approaches. Dr. Wallach's assertion challenges the notion that disease management must be complex and costly, advocating instead for a return to fundamental principles of nutrition and supplementation.

Central to Dr. Wallach's philosophy is the belief that "All disease is from lack of vitamins and minerals." This bold statement encapsulates his fundamental thesis: that deficiencies in essential nutrients underlie the majority of health ailments. Moreover, Dr. Wallach contends that modern food production practices have contributed to a decline in the nutritional quality of our diets, stating, "Our foods don't have any nutrients anymore; that's why we get sick."

Dr. Wallach and Ma Lan, authors of "Rare Earths, Forbidden Cures," reveal the historical significance of silver in healthcare, tracing its usage back thousands of years. Silver may function as a systemic disinfectant supporting the immune system, as it contributes to overall health and longevity.

Your Body Needs Silver

Researchers have recently uncovered a startling trend: a significant decline in the silver content of foods like fruits and vegetables since the 1940s. This decline raises questions about the potential impact on human health and immunity.

Wayne Rowland commonly draws attention to the agricultural practices that contribute to the depletion of nutrient content in food, stating, "And the more fertilizers they use and the more craziness that they use in the soil, the more stuff that they do, the less nutrient value is in that food, the less colloids are in that food for you to utilize."

Historical data indicates that food crops, particularly grains, fruits, and vegetables, contained much higher levels of silver decades ago. Early clinical studies, such as one conducted in 1940 by R.A. Kehoe of UCLA, estimated that the average daily intake of silver from fruits and vegetables provided between 50-100 mcg as trace elements.

However, by 1975, the silver content in our diets, including food and water, had plummeted to deficient levels. Interestingly enough, measurements of silver content shifted from micrograms to picograms, delineating the drastic reduction in silver intake over just a few decades.

A comprehensive analysis published in 1989 revealed that silver was no longer even mentioned as a trace element in food. This decline in dietary silver raises concerns about its implications for human health.

While the FDA maintains no proven relationship between silver intake and improved health, some researchers, like Dr. Robert O. Becker, M.D., argue otherwise. Dr. Becker's research into the healing benefits of colloidal silver led him to believe that low silver levels in the body may contribute to increased susceptibility to illness and disease.

Clinical studies have shown that silver plays a role in boosting immunity by enhancing the infection-fighting capacity of white blood cells while increasing the production of oxygen-carrying red blood cells, not to mention silver's ability to act as an effective antimicrobial agent, effectively combating pathogens.

Given these findings, many researchers suggest that higher levels of silver in food and water in the past helped maintain overall health and protected us from infectious diseases. The decline in dietary silver supports the importance of further investigation into the role of trace minerals in human health and the potential benefits of supplementing with silver to support immunity, increased health, quality of life, and longevity.

In addressing the pressing issue of the influx of drugs and chemicals into our food supply, Wayne Rowland emphasizes the urgent need for action. He highlights the detrimental impact of these substances on human health, explaining, "All the drugs and chemicals, fertilizers, and such that get into the plant via soil, air, and water find their way into your body, and this drags your vibration down." This lowering of the vibratory rate creates an environment conducive to the proliferation of parasites, contributing to even more health problems.

Rowland advocates for a proactive approach to address this issue, stressing the importance of detoxification to cleanse the body of harmful substances. He asserts, "We need to clean up. We need to do it. We need to flush the body out with something that will work." Urgency is necessary, reasonable, and prudent in tackling disease and mitigating the adverse effects of environmental toxins.

Then, there are the broader repercussions of environmental contamination, attributing various global challenges to the prevalence of filth. Wayne urges concerted efforts to address these underlying issues, stating, "There are all kinds of things happening on this planet that are not so good, and it's being caused by filth." His call to action urges the need for proactive collective responsibility in safeguarding human and environmental health.

The Growing Case for Silver

Research has indicated a potential link between silver deficiency and compromised immunity, shedding light on the vital role of silver in maintaining overall health. Dr. Becker notes a correlation between low silver levels and prolonged illnesses. His studies suggested that a deficiency in silver could impair immune function, contributing to prolonged illness duration.

In his book "The Body Electric" and other writings, Dr. Becker highlighted the immune-stimulating properties of silver, suggesting that it plays a crucial role beyond merely killing disease-causing organisms. He observed that silver promoted tissue growth and regeneration, accelerating healing in burn patients and elderly individuals. Moreover, Dr.

Becker's research indicated that silver could induce the transformation of cancer cells into normal cells, offering promising implications for cancer treatment.

Studies conducted throughout the early 1900s documented its efficacy in combating various infections, leading to widespread use in hospitals and laboratories worldwide.

Numerous experts in the medical field have attested to the health benefits of colloidal silver, shedding light on its potential to enhance immune function and combat infections. Dr. Jonathan V. Wright, M.D., from the esteemed Tahoma Clinic in Washington State, emphasizes that silver can improve the ability of white blood cells to eradicate germs. Highlighting research from the Journal of the American Medical Association dating back to 1909, Dr. Wright explains how colloidal silver increases immune cells' effectiveness in destroying pathogens.

Clinical researcher V. Edwards-Jones, writing in "Letters in Applied Microbiology," discusses the antimicrobial properties of silver, noting its efficacy in reducing bio-burden and preventing infections. The use of silver nanoparticles shows promise in enhancing antimicrobial activity and potentially modulating immune responses.

The Food and Drug Administration

Colloidal silver has gained attention recently for its purported health and healing capabilities. Advocates tout colloidal silver's antimicrobial properties and potential benefits for various ailments. However, despite its popularity in some circles, the widespread use of colloidal silver remains limited, with regulatory hurdles and pharmaceutical industry influence playing significant roles in its restricted access.

The U.S. Food and Drug Administration (FDA) serves as the regulatory authority overseeing the safety and efficacy of medical products, including dietary supplements like colloidal silver. While colloidal silver is legally available as a dietary supplement, the FDA heavily regulates its marketing claims. This regulatory stance stems from concerns about potential side effects and unsubstantiated health claims.

One of the primary challenges facing colloidal silver's widespread use is the need for comprehensive scientific evidence supporting its efficacy and safety for various health conditions. While some studies suggest potential antimicrobial properties, much of the existing research is limited in scope and quality. The FDA requires robust clinical data to support health claims, and with such evidence, marketing colloidal silver for medical purposes becomes legally secure.

The FDA regulates colloidal silver as a dietary supplement rather than a pharmaceutical drug. This classification subjects it to different regulatory standards, further complicating its path to mainstream acceptance in medical practice. Pharmaceutical companies, which invest heavily in research and development to bring drugs to market, may view colloidal silver as a potential competitor or threat to their revenue streams.

The influence of pharmaceutical companies extends beyond direct competition. These companies often have significant lobbying power and financial resources, enabling them to shape regulatory policies and public perceptions of alternative therapies like colloidal silver. Skepticism or downplaying of colloidal silver's potential benefits may align with their interests in maintaining dominance in the healthcare market.

The financial considerations surrounding medical treatments are crucial in shaping healthcare decisions. While colloidal silver may offer potential health benefits, its use in medical treatments may not always align with the profit-driven motives of pharmaceutical companies and the bankers who support them. Developing and marketing pharmaceutical drugs can be lucrative, with substantial returns on investment. In contrast, natural remedies like colloidal silver offer less profitable opportunities, particularly since they cannot be patented or monetized in the same way as proprietary drugs.

Critics argue that the regulatory framework and pharmaceutical industry influence create barriers to accessing alternative therapies like colloidal silver, limiting consumer choice and potentially depriving individuals of potentially beneficial treatments. They advocate for more significant research funding and regulatory flexibility to explore the therapeutic potential of colloidal silver and other natural remedies.

The FDA, the government relations branch of the pharmaceutical drug cartel, as the regulatory body overseeing pharmaceuticals, has issued public advisories cautioning against the use of colloidal silver. They maintain insufficient scientific evidence or research to definitively establish the safety and efficacy of colloidal silver. This caution is outlined in the Department of Health and Human Services (HHS) regulations [HHS – Food and Drug Administration, 21 CFR Part 310, Docket No. 96N-0144], explicitly addressing over-the-counter drug products containing colloidal silver ingredients or silver salts.

The absence of comprehensive scientific studies on colloidal silver's safety and effectiveness can be attributed to a lack of funding from pharmaceutical companies. Given that pharmaceutical companies typically finance research for products with profit potential, there has been limited investment in conducting rigorous scientific investigations into colloidal silver simply because there is no money to be made from promoting colloidal silver.

It is easy to ignore thousands of years of physical success using silver as the main antibiotic because it has been too successful to suit the aims of the current medical monopoly.

Additionally, despite historical evidence showcasing colloidal silver's effectiveness as a natural antibiotic over thousands of years, it has been largely overlooked by the modern medical establishment. The success of colloidal silver challenges the interests of the current medical system, potentially impacting the demand for pharmaceutical antibiotics and other treatments.

In essence, the FDA's warnings regarding colloidal silver reflect the wealth of well-funded scientific research in this area and a reluctance within the medical community to acknowledge alternative inexpensive treatments that may compete with conventional pharmaceuticals.

Despite its historical efficacy, colloidal silver remains a contentious subject within the medical field, even though it is welcomed with open arms by most self-reliant individuals who rely on results for their treatment choices.

It Comes Down to This

Wayne Rowland urgently cautions, "I'm telling you, this is big stuff, and now the FDA is on to us," he declares, "They now know what Silver Water will do; they now know what all this stuff is doing."

Wayne Rowland concludes:

The FDA is strongarming and prescriptionalizing everything; if they have their way, you won't be able to buy colloidal silver; you will not be able to read these words or hear us speak by this time next year.

Nobody will be able to tell you the truth because the FDA is shutting it all down with a new program they've put in motion. They've declared war and made it a labeling issue, and they're taking all colloids off the market, but I'm ready for them. I've taken the precautions to reformat Silver Water to be classified as a healthy drinking water alternative so you can still get the product.

The FDA falsifies reports like some 75-year-old woman when she was 13 years old said she drank some colloidal silver and turned blue. No one in the history of anything has ever turned blue from it.

This suspension of your rights means you cannot go to the health food store and read about what you're buying. You can't read about it; you won't be able to walk in and buy colloidal silver in a store, even though it does wonders for you.

We as a country have let this go on for far too long and haven't done anything about it, and if you want to do something about it, you better start doing something now because this is a huge issue.

I can sell ionic mineral drinking water, so you'll still be able to buy the product, but we will never again be able to exercise our rights of free speech to write or talk about it. Communism is here.

I've done the absolute best I can, folks, and I tell you right now, I can get your health back, but from here on out, it's up to you.

You have to take it from here.

~ Wayne Rowland

For more information visit www.waynerowland.com

NOTES:

Made in the USA
Columbia, SC
30 January 2025

53000758R00061